God Bless
May 2024

Let's Learn
about
The Rosary!

It's near the end of the day and everything looks so beautiful that I want to take some time to just visit with God and get close to Him.

And what better way to do so than by means of the Rosary?

As we pray the Rosary, the Mysteries tell us what to meditate on—what to think about—as we say our prayers.

As we do this, we will grow closer to Christ and to His blessed Mother.

This will show you how to pray the Rosary. Begin with:

1 **THE SIGN OF THE CROSS**

In the name of the Father and of the Son and of the Holy Spirit. Amen.

THE APOSTLES' CREED

I believe in God, the Father almighty, Creator of Heaven and earth; and in Jesus Christ, His only Son, our Lord, who was conceived by the Holy Spirit, born of the Virgin Mary, suffered under Pontius Pilate, was crucified, died, and was buried. He descended into Hell; the third day He rose again from the dead; He ascended into Heaven, and sitteth at the right hand of God, the Father almighty; from thence He shall come to judge the living and the dead.

I believe in the Holy Spirit, the holy Catholic Church, the communion of saints, the forgiveness of sins, the resurrection of the body and life everlasting. Amen.

2 **OUR FATHER**

Our Father who art in heaven, hallowed be Thy name. Thy kingdom come. Thy will be done on earth, as it is in heaven.

Give us this day our daily bread, and forgive us our trespasses, as we forgive those who trespass against us, and lead us not into temptation, but deliver us from evil. Amen.

3 And now we pray one Hail Mary that we may grow in **faith**, another that we'll grow in **hope,** and still another that we'll grow in **charity**; which means to grow in love for God and others!

THE HAIL MARY

Hail Mary, full of grace, the Lord is with thee. Blessed art thou amongst women. And blessed is the fruit of thy womb: Jesus. Holy Mary, Mother of God, pray for us sinners, now and at the hour of our death. Amen.

4   **ANNOUNCE THE FIRST MYSTERY / SAY ONE "OUR FATHER"**

5   **SAY TEN "HAIL MARYS" WHILE THINKING ABOUT THE MYSTERY AND THEN SAY:**

THE GLORY BE

Glory be to the Father and to the Son and to the Holy Spirit. As it was in the beginning, is now and ever shall be, world without end. Amen.

THE FATIMA PRAYER

Oh my Jesus, forgive us our sins. Save us from the fires of hell. Lead all souls to heaven, especially those who are most in need of Thy mercy.

6   **ANNOUNCE THE SECOND MYSTERY / SAY ONE "OUR FATHER"**

7   **SAY TEN "HAIL MARYS" WHILE THINKING ABOUT THE MYSTERY AND THEN ONE "GLORY BE" AND ONE "FATIMA PRAYER"**

8   **ANNOUNCE THE THIRD MYSTERY / SAY ONE "OUR FATHER"**

9   **SAY TEN "HAIL MARYS" WHILE THINKING ABOUT THE MYSTERY AND THEN ONE "GLORY BE" AND ONE "FATIMA PRAYER"**

10   **ANNOUNCE THE FOURTH MYSTERY / SAY ONE "OUR FATHER"**

11   **SAY TEN "HAIL MARYS" WHILE THINKING ABOUT THE MYSTERY AND THEN ONE "GLORY BE" AND ONE "FATIMA PRAYER"**

12   **ANNOUNCE THE FIFTH MYSTERY / SAY ONE "OUR FATHER"**

13   **SAY TEN "HAIL MARYS" WHILE THINKING ABOUT THE MYSTERY AND THEN ONE "GLORY BE" AND ONE "FATIMA PRAYER"**

CLOSING PRAYERS:

Hail, Holy Queen, Mother of mercy, our life, our sweetness, and our hope. To thee do we cry, poor banished children of Eve, to thee do we send up our sighs, mourning and weeping in this valley of tears. Turn then, most gracious advocate, thine eyes of mercy toward us; and after this our exile show unto us the blessed fruit of Thy womb, Jesus. O clement, O loving, O sweet Virgin Mary.

Pray for us, O holy Mother of God. That we may be made worthy of the promises of Christ.

O God, whose only begotten Son, by His life, death, and resurrection, has purchased for us the rewards of eternal salvation; grant, we beseech Thee, that meditating upon these mysteries of the most holy Rosary of the Blessed Virgin Mary, we may imitate what they contain and obtain what they promise, through the same Christ our Lord. Amen.

In the name of the Father and of the Son and of the Holy Spirit. Amen.

You can pray the mysteries on the following days:

Monday: Joyful
Tuesday: Sorrowful
Wednesday: Glorious
Thursday: Luminous
Friday: Sorrowful
Saturday: Joyful
Sunday: Glorious

As we pray, we think about different things that happened in the lives of Jesus and Mary, and as a result, it brings our heart close to theirs.

Do you want to join me?

Let's stop thinking about all the other things we want to do and let's spend this time with God.

THE JOYFUL MYSTERIES

The birth and early life of Jesus

The Annunciation

MEDITATION

In a small town in Israel, a young girl of about 15 is startled to see an angel. He says, "Hail, full of grace! The Lord is with you!" And then he tells her that she has been chosen to be the mother of God's Son. Young Mary listens closely and then replies, "I am the handmaiden of the Lord. Let it be done as God pleases." What love of God!

PRAYER

Jesus, when You ask anything of me, help me be humble like Your mother and always say yes. Amen.

PRAY:

1 Our Father

10 Hail Marys

1 Glory Be

The Visitation

MEDITATION

Full of joy at what the angel told her, Mary rushes to visit her cousin, Elizabeth. The angel had also told Mary that Elizabeth is expecting a child. The two women meet and Elizabeth exclaims: "From now on, all people will call you blessed!"

PRAYER

Dear Mary, help me be as joyful doing God's will as you are.

PRAY:

1 Our Father

10 Hail Marys

1 Glory Be

The Nativity

MEDITATION

God has chosen Joseph to be the earthly father of Jesus. Together, Mary and Joseph travel to Bethlehem in obedience to the local law. They are tired after the long trip, and then Mary feels her baby is about to be born! Bethlehem is full of many visitors. There is only one place for the baby to be born: a stable that houses animals. And there, the humble family welcomes the Son of God.

PRAYER

Dear Lord, help me remember that the way You work in my life may be very different from the way I think things should be.

PRAY:

1 Our Father

10 Hail Marys

1 Glory Be

The Presentation

MEDITATION

Eight days later, Joseph and Mary take baby Jesus to the temple to dedicate Him to God. An old prophet named Simeon sees them and comes near. He tells them that their son is the savior of the world. Then he tells Mary that she will have many sorrows. Mary has always said yes to God and she says yes again, even if it means she will have pain at what is to come.

PRAYER

O God, Mary had faith in You in everything. Help me never to doubt what You want in my life.

PRAY:

1 Our Father

10 Hail Marys

1 Glory Be

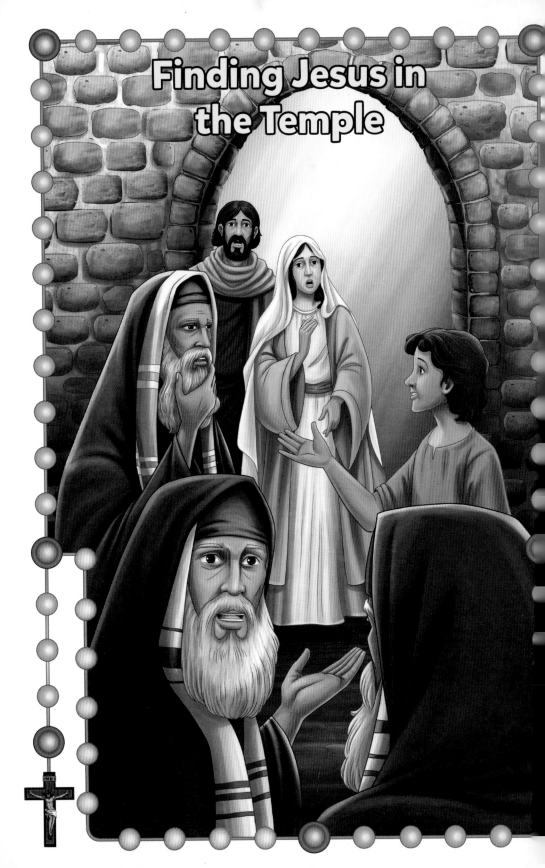

Finding Jesus in the Temple

MEDITATION

It is twelve years later, and the Holy Family has gone to visit the temple. A few days later, after visiting Jerusalem, Joseph and Mary begin the long trip home when they realize that Jesus is not with the caravan. They rush back to the city and look for Him. After three days they find Him in the temple sitting with the teachers, who are amazed at His understanding.

"Didn't you realize I would be in my Father's house?" Jesus asked His parents. Then He returned and continued to be obedient to them.

PRAYER

Dear Jesus, as a child, You were obedient to those that cared for You. Help me do the same.

PRAY:

1 Our Father

10 Hail Marys

1 Glory Be

You can pray the mysteries on the following days:

Monday: Joyful
Tuesday: Sorrowful
Wednesday: Glorious
Thursday: Luminous
Friday: Sorrowful
Saturday: Joyful
Sunday: Glorious

As we pray, we think about different things that happened in the lives of Jesus and Mary, and as a result, it brings our heart close to theirs.

Do you want to join me?

Let's stop thinking about all the other things we want to do and let's spend this time with God.

THE LUMINOUS MYSTERIES

Jesus shares the good news of the gospel!

The Baptism of Jesus

MEDITATION

When Jesus is 30 years old, right before He begins His work among the people, He goes to the Jordan River to be baptized by His cousin, John. As Jesus comes up out of the water, the Spirit of God comes down upon Him like a dove and a voice is heard from Heaven saying: This is My beloved Son in whom I am well pleased.

PRAYER

Dear Jesus, You always pleased the Father. You know I am not perfect, but help me to do my best to be close to Him and to follow His ways.

PRAY:

1 Our Father

10 Hail Marys

1 Glory Be

The Wedding at Cana

MEDITATION

Jesus, His mother and some of His followers have been invited to a wedding. Suddenly Mary realizes that the wedding couple have run out of wine for their guests. She shares the problem with her son and Jesus turns water into wine.

PRAYER

Dear Mary, you were concerned about people's needs. I know you are concerned with mine. Help me to bring all my needs to God in prayer, as well as the needs of others.

PRAY:

1 Our Father

10 Hail Marys

1 Glory Be

The Proclamation of the Kingdom

MEDITATION

Jesus begins to share the good news of the coming kingdom. He heals the blind, the people that can't walk, the people that can't speak, and He even brings people back to life from the dead. People are amazed! God has come to them through His Son!

PRAYER

Dear Jesus, in You is all hope and in You is everything I need in life. You can help us now just like You did people in the past. Help me to believe that and to share that good news with others.

PRAY:

1 Our Father

10 Hail Marys

1 Glory Be

The Transfiguration

MEDITATION

Jesus goes up a mountain, taking His disciples Peter, James and John. Once there, the disciples see Jesus shining with great splendor and speaking with two prophets who had died long ago. The disciples are amazed! God has blessed them with this wonderful sight of Jesus in His glory.

PRAYER

Lord Jesus, help me remember that by following You, I am serving a powerful and glorious God. All power and glory is Yours!

PRAY:

1 Our Father

10 Hail Marys

1 Glory Be

The Last Supper

MEDITATION

Jesus is having the last supper with his disciples. He knows that very soon He will suffer in a great way. He knows He will be taken away and crucified. He doesn't want to leave His disciples alone. He takes bread, blesses it and says: "This is My body." He takes wine, blesses it, and says, "This is My blood."

PRAYER

Lord, You are with me always through Communion. Help me never forget that You gave Your life for me.

PRAY:

1 Our Father

10 Hail Marys

1 Glory Be

You can pray the mysteries on the following days:

Monday: Joyful
Tuesday: Sorrowful
Wednesday: Glorious
Thursday: Luminous
Friday: Sorrowful
Saturday: Joyful
Sunday: Glorious

As we pray, we think about different things that happened in the lives of Jesus and Mary, and as a result, it brings our heart close to theirs.

Do you want to join me?

Let's stop thinking about all the other things we want to do and let's spend this time with God.

THE SORROWFUL MYSTERIES

The suffering and death of Jesus Christ for you and me

The Agony in The Garden

MEDITATION

The last supper has ended, and knowing what is to come, Jesus takes some of His disciples to the Garden of Gethsemane. It is late and His disciples fall asleep while Jesus prays. He is afraid of what is to come, but He says yes to His Father's will. Jesus suffers for us.

PRAYER

O Father, let me not forget how much Jesus gave of Himself for me and for all people. Let me never think I am better than others.

PRAY:

1 Our Father

10 Hail Marys

1 Glory Be

The Scourging at the Pillar

MEDITATION

The soldiers come to the garden. They take Jesus by force and He is accused of many things. Jesus, who healed the sick and raised the dead—the one who fed thousands of people and taught them about God's ways—is now tied to a pillar... and whipped.

PRAYER

O Lord, how great is Your love for us. Help me never doubt it.

PRAY:

1 Our Father

10 Hail Marys

1 Glory Be

The Crowning with Thorns

MEDITATION

While He's still bleeding from the whip, the Roman soldiers make fun of Jesus. They hit Him and make Him feel worse. They put a purple cloth around His shoulders and they make a crown of sharp thorns and place it on His head. They do not show mercy.

PRAYER

Dear Jesus, even today many people say bad things about You, not realizing who You really are. Help more people to know You and what You have done for the salvation of the world.

PRAY:

1 Our Father

10 Hail Marys

1 Glory Be

Carrying the Cross

MEDITATION

After a night of a lot of pain and being made fun of and mistreated, a heavy wooden cross is placed on Jesus' back. Then He is made to carry it up to the place where He is to be put to death. Tired and in pain, He falls three times. Each time He is made to get up. With difficulty, Jesus makes His way to the top of Golgotha.

PRAYER

Dear God, whenever I get discouraged, let me remember how You got back up out of love for all people.

PRAY:

1 Our Father

10 Hail Marys

1 Glory Be

The Crucifixion

MEDITATION

Jesus reaches the top of Golgotha. He is placed on the cross between two thieves. He forgives the men that did all this to Him saying, "Father, they do not know what they are doing." Jesus suffers, and after some time, He says, "It is finished." He dies for our sins.

Jesus died on the cross for you and me.

PRAYER

Dear Lord, let me never look at a cross the same again. Let me look at the cross and remember every step You took for me.

PRAY:

1 Our Father

10 Hail Marys

1 Glory Be

You can pray the mysteries on the following days:

Monday: Joyful
Tuesday: Sorrowful
Wednesday: Glorious
Thursday: Luminous
Friday: Sorrowful
Saturday: Joyful
Sunday: Glorious

As we pray, we think about different things that happened in the lives of Jesus and Mary, and as a result, it brings our heart close to theirs.

Do you want to join me?

Let's stop thinking about all the other things we want to do and let's spend this time with God.

THE GLORIOUS MYSTERIES

Death cannot hold God's Son! Jesus rises from the dead and shows us the hope of Heaven!

The Resurrection

MEDITATION

Three days after the death of Christ, His apostles are in hiding because they are afraid. But at the tomb where the body of Jesus lies, something happens. There is an earthquake, the stone covering the entrance rolls away, and suddenly Jesus comes out. He has risen! He is alive!

PRAYER

Dear Lord, how wonderful that not even death can stop You! You have made a way for us to Heaven!

PRAY:

1 Our Father

10 Hail Marys

1 Glory Be

The Ascension

MEDITATION

After His resurrection, Jesus spends 40 days with His disciples, teaching and encouraging them. "You will receive power when the Holy Spirit comes upon you and then you will go to all the world and tell others about Me." As He speaks with them, Jesus ascends until He is hidden by a cloud. Then two angels appear and say, "Why are you looking at the sky? In the same way Jesus was taken from you, He will return."

PRAYER

Jesus, You have gone to heaven to prepare a way for us. You are at the right hand of God. Help me to be ready for Your coming!

PRAY:

1 Our Father

10 Hail Marys

1 Glory Be

The Descent of The Holy Spirit

MEDITATION

Before Jesus ascended, He told His disciples to wait in the city until He would send them the Holy Spirit. Then one day, as the disciples prayed, there is the sound of a rushing wind, and tongues of fire appear over them. The disciples' hearts are overflowing and praising God! They are ready to go into all the world and be witnesses for Jesus!

PRAYER

Dear Jesus, You sent Your Holy Spirit to Your Church. Fill me with an overflowing joy that I may point more people to You.

PRAY:

1 Our Father

10 Hail Marys

1 Glory Be

The Assumption

MEDITATION

The Virgin Mary has completed what God wanted her to do on earth. She has been faithful to God's will and now it is time for her to join Jesus in Heaven. God takes her, body and soul, into glory! She has gone home to God just as one day we shall, too.

PRAYER

Dear Mary, you are mother to Jesus. You are also my mother in Heaven. What a wonderful thought!

PRAY:

1 Our Father

10 Hail Marys

1 Glory Be

The Coronation

MEDITATION

A wonder appears in Heaven: a woman clothed with the sun, with the moon under her feet, and on her head a crown of 12 stars. And she gave birth to a son who is to rule all nations. Mary lived to bring Jesus into the world; now Jesus gives honor to His mother. Mary is Queen of Heaven.

PRAYER

Blessed Mother and Queen of Heaven, please pray for me and help me do my best to stay close to Jesus.

PRAY:

1 Our Father

10 Hail Marys

1 Glory Be

Pray the following after you have finished praying the Rosary:

HAIL, HOLY QUEEN

Hail, holy Queen, mother of mercy, our life, our sweetness, and our hope. To thee do we cry, poor banished children of Eve. To thee do we send up our sighs, mourning and weeping in this valley of tears. Turn then, most gracious advocate, thine eyes of mercy toward us, and after this our exile show us the blessed fruit of thy womb, Jesus. O clement, O loving, O sweet Virgin Mary.

Pray for us, O Holy Mother of God.

That we may be made worthy of the promises of Christ.

Let us pray.

O God, whose only begotten Son, by His life, death, and resurrection, has purchased for us the rewards of eternal salvation: grant, we beseech Thee, that while meditating on these mysteries of the most holy Rosary of the Blessed Virgin Mary, that we may both imitate what they contain and obtain what they promise, through Christ our Lord. Amen.

Most Sacred Heart of Jesus, have mercy on us.

Immaculate Heart of Mary, pray for us.

In the name of the Father and of the Son and of the Holy Spirit

Amen.

Go to the Madonna. Love her!
Always say the Rosary. Say it well.
Say it as often as you can!
Be souls of prayer. Never tire
of praying, it is what is essential.
Prayer shakes the Heart of God
and obtains necessary Graces!

~Saint Padre Pio